THE
PROJECT

Copyright © 2025 by Justin Balee Williams

Published by Kudu

All rights reserved. No portion of this book may be reproduced, stored in a retrieval system, or transmitted in any form or by any means—electronic, mechanical, photocopy, recording, scanning, or other—except for brief quotations in critical reviews or articles, without prior written permission of the author.

Unless otherwise specified, all Scripture quotations are taken from the CSB Christian Standard Bible, Copyright © 2017 by Holman Bible Publishers. Used by permission. Christian Standard Bible® and CSB® are federally registered trademarks of Holman Bible Publishers, all rights reserved | Scripture quotations marked NIV are taken from the Holy Bible, New International Version®, NIV®. Copyright © 1973, 1978, 1984, 2011 by Biblica, Inc.™ Used by permission of Zondervan. All rights reserved worldwide. www.zondervan.com. The "NIV" and "New International Version" are trademarks registered in the United States Patent and Trademark Office by Biblica, Inc.™

For foreign and subsidiary rights, contact the author.

Cover design by: Sara Young
Cover photo by: Elijah Benjamin Williams

Photo Credits: All photographs in this book were taken by and are the property of Justin Williams. Unauthorized use or reproduction is prohibited.

ISBN: 978-1-962401-11-1   1 2 3 4 5 6 7 8 9 10

Printed in the United States of America

**CHANGING LIVES
ONE MEAL AT A TIME**

THE PROJECT

JUSTIN BALEE WILLIAMS

This book is dedicated to all the forgotten children who have endured the harsh realities of starvation and poverty.

CONTENTS

Acknowledgments.. xiii

Introduction 15

CHAPTER 1. **The Beginning**........................... 23

CHAPTER 2. **The Call**................................... 35

CHAPTER 3. **The Destruction**......................... 49

CHAPTER 4. **The Moment**............................. 67

CHAPTER 5. **The Plate Project** 75

Resources...89

Photos 93

ACKNOWLEDGMENTS

To my beautiful family, who inspire me daily and give me my true purpose—my love for you is forever and always.

INTRODUCTION

Have you ever found yourself stepping into something entirely new—a moment when everything around you feels unfamiliar, yet strangely right? Maybe it was starting a new job, moving to a different city, or standing on the edge of an experience that would change you forever. That mix of nervous anticipation and quiet certainty that you're exactly where you're meant to be. For me, that moment came when I boarded a plane to Haiti.

Haiti isn't just a place on a map to me—it's a piece of my soul. It's the land where my father was born, the home of half my family, and the spark that ignited my passion for truly loving people. Growing up, I often sat at my father's feet, listening to stories about his childhood in an orphanage in Pétion-Ville. His memories were a mosaic of hardship, resilience, and hope. Those stories shaped me long before I ever set foot on Haitian soil, planting seeds of purpose that would eventually take root in ways I could never have imagined.

My father's story is one of incredible resilience. Born in one of the poorest countries in the world, he began his life with an unimaginable challenge. On the day he was

THE PROJECT

born, my grandparents noticed a golf ball-sized mass on his lip—a hemangioma. Without access to proper medical care, my grandparents faced a gut-wrenching decision. In a place like Haiti, where survival was already uncertain, they feared for their son's future. In their community, it wasn't unheard of to let go of a child born with such a burden to spare them from a life of suffering. But my grandparents didn't see a burden in their newborn son; they saw life. Despite having no idea how they would care for him or get him the medical help he needed, they chose to keep him, trusting God to provide a way.

As my father grew, the hemangioma worsened. Every day, he bled. The local clinic could no longer help him, and once again, my grandparents were faced with a devastating reality—there was nothing they could do. That's when they heard about the Haiti Christian Orphanage, a place they were told might be able to save their son's life. In desperation, they made the painful decision to give him up, praying that this orphanage would be the safe haven he needed. My grandfather, with a few belongings packed, began the grueling two-day journey on foot, carrying his son to a place they hoped would offer a future.

INTRODUCTION

The way my dad tells the story of being dropped off at the orphanage never fails to break me. I've heard it countless times, but picturing my father, just six years old, bleeding to death in front of strangers is almost incomprehensible. As a father myself, I can't imagine being faced with such a decision—saving my child's life at the cost of not being in it. That's what my grandparents had to do. My father still remembers that day like it was yesterday—the moment he saw his own father walking away, leaving him behind. He ran after him, tears streaming down his little face, his voice trembling as he cried out, "Daddy, don't leave me!" His father stopped, turned, and knelt down. He picked up his son, held him tightly. He looked into his son's tear-filled eyes, memorizing every detail, as if trying to etch this moment into his heart forever. Then, with a deep breath, he set him down, whispered goodbye, and turned away. My father watched as his figure grew smaller, step by step, until he disappeared.

My father was left alone, with nothing but the weight of uncertainty. I can't begin to fathom the fear he felt at that moment.

THE PROJECT

Yet, as heartbreaking as that story is, what happened next is nothing short of a miracle. That very night, after my father had been dropped off at the orphanage, one of the few surgeons in the world who could perform the life-saving surgery he needed happened to be visiting the orphanage. Within months, my father was on a plane to the United States for the surgery that would save his life. His operation was a success, and the rest is part of a story that has shaped not just his life but mine as well.

My grandfather's sacrifice taught me the true meaning of being a father—a protector, a provider, someone willing to do whatever it takes for the sake of their child. He laid down his pride and gave his son over to God, trusting that if it was God's will, my father's life would be saved. My grandfather's faith laid a foundation for every generation to come. And that faith—his belief that life is more than the circumstances we are born into, that we are all *projects*, part of something greater—has become the core of who I am becoming.

I invite you to join me on a journey—a reflection on a mission that has profoundly shaped my heart and soul.

INTRODUCTION

It's a story of immense joy and the weighty responsibility that comes with answering the call to serve, love, and illuminate even the darkest corners of the world. It's a testament to the profound truth that our lives are brimming with purpose, that every breath we draw carries the promise of resilience and untapped potential, and that we each have a unique role in this greater narrative we call life.

So, let us return to where it all began. . . .

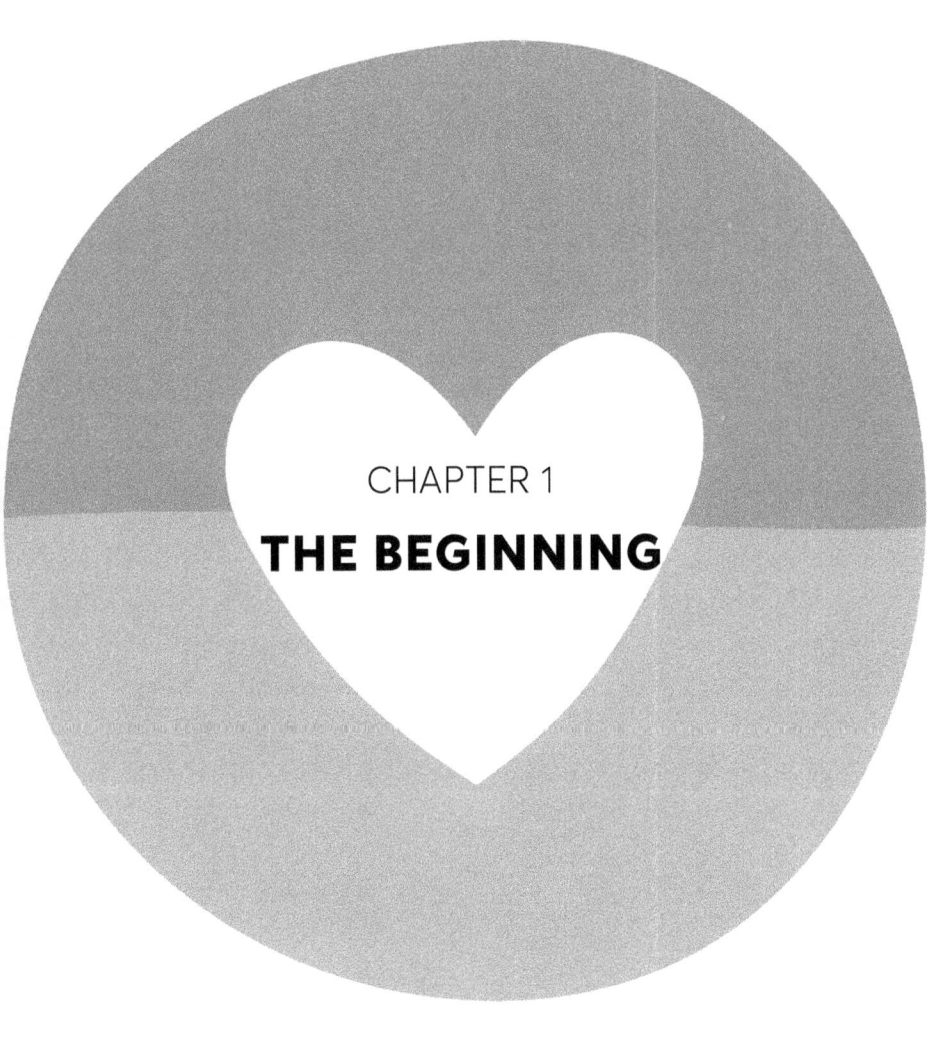

CHAPTER 1
THE BEGINNING

THE BEGINNING

I've had the privilege of living quite an interesting life, filled with adventures that have granted me access to incredible experiences. I've witnessed the hand of God intricately woven into the lives of His people and have seen His grace in action. But, at the same time, I'm a bit of a *project*. I've also encountered hardships—challenges that made me question everything and caused me to wonder about the nature of life and faith itself.

Growing up, my upbringing was quite different from that of the average child. Both of my parents were survivors, each with their own remarkable story, which imbued our family life with a sense of adventure. My parents are undoubtedly the most incredible people I have ever known. Their lives are a testament to sacrifice, dedicated to serving Jesus and His kingdom.

From them, I learned the importance of serving others—a lesson that shaped the very core of my love for people.

Have you ever felt like life was pulling you toward something bigger than yourself? That sense of purpose, the tug that makes you want to live for more than just the

THE PROJECT

daily grind? Those who embrace this feeling—like my grandparents, my parents, and many others—often live with a sense of purpose that extends far beyond their own needs or desires. They recognize that their life is part of a much bigger story, and they draw strength from that.

It's like sailing a ship. When you're out on the open sea, you can easily drift without direction, but once you set your sails toward a destination, every wind, every current, and every challenge has meaning. You're no longer drifting—you're on a mission. That sense of being anchored to a purpose, guided by a greater cause, propels you forward with resilience and focus. When we live for something beyond ourselves, we unlock an inner strength and joy that carry us through even the toughest storms in life.

For me, this isn't just an idea—it's deeply personal. It's one of the reasons I'm alive today and why I feel so passionate about sharing this message with you. I've been blessed with incredible examples of this kind of living.

THE BEGINNING

But my personal journey has been complex. While I've had amazing role models, that doesn't mean I was always ready to accept the mission. I've been through a lot, made countless mistakes, and fallen short in more ways than I can count. Even with great examples to follow, until there's a true revelation in your own heart, mind, and soul, it all comes and goes. And trust me, life definitely came and went for me in my walk with Jesus. I want to be clear—I'm not writing this from the perspective of someone who has it all figured out. Not at all. I'm constantly becoming, and I pray that my transformation continues until the day of glory. What I can do, though, is share the passion and conviction I believe I was made for.

You see, my mother was never supposed to have children. This was one of the hardest realities my parents had to face early in their marriage. But within just three months into their marriage, they received a miracle—a surprise they didn't expect. I was that miracle, defying what doctors had told them. And the miracles didn't stop there. In so many ways, I shouldn't be here.

THE PROJECT

Let me take you back to a day in April 1999 that started like any other.

The sun was shining, and the air was electric with the laughter and shouts of kids excited by a makeshift bike ramp—a rickety construction of random objects that promised more danger than stability. Yet, to us, it was an irresistible challenge.

Caught up in the excitement, I decided to be the first to tackle the ramp. My heart was racing as I pedaled harder and faster, my friends' cheers becoming a distant echo. As I approached the ramp, a surge of adrenaline coursed through my veins. I hit the base of the ramp with all the force I could muster, launching into the air. For a split second, I felt like I was flying. But that moment of exhilaration quickly turned to terror as I realized I had lost control. The handlebars wobbled violently beneath my grip, and my front wheel twisted sideways.

Mid-air, I felt the bike slipping away from me. Time seemed to slow as I hung in the balance between earth and sky, my stomach plummeting with the realization of the impending crash. My body twisted awkwardly, and

THE BEGINNING

I was powerless to correct my trajectory. The ground rushed up to meet me with brutal speed.

I landed face-first on the unforgiving concrete of my neighbor's driveway. Pain exploded in my skull, and my vision darkened at the edges. My body crumpled like a ragdoll, and I lay there, motionless, the jagged edges of the concrete scraping against my skin.

The next moments were a blur of chaos and agony. I could feel my consciousness slipping.

Through my hazy vision, I saw my mother running towards me—her face a mask of sheer terror—calling 911. Her screams pierced the air, a desperate cry for help that seemed to echo into infinity.

As a father now, I can hardly bear the weight of what she must have felt. Watching the paramedics call for an emergency airlift, knowing that each moment could be my last, brought a terrifying clarity: When the situation worsened and I began to convulse, my mother did what she knew best—she prayed. For those who don't know my mother, let me paint a picture: she is a spirit-filled

THE PROJECT

prayer warrior. If ever there was someone to turn to in need of prayer, she is that woman. Kneeling beside me, she laid her hands on me and pleaded fervently with Jesus to heal her son.

The power of prayer is immense, especially when paired with genuine faith. My mother believed wholeheartedly in the promises of Jesus, and in that critical moment, her faith was not in vain. Jesus answered. Miraculously, every aspect of my being—mind, body, and spirit—was restored. My bodily functions normalized so abruptly that I even began to engage in conversations, bewildering everyone around me with my sudden recovery.

The paramedics were at a loss. One moment, a child lay dying before them; the next, he was completely healed, with no medical explanation other than a divine intervention. That was the conclusion they had to relay when they called off the emergency airlift that was supposed to save my life.

Despite the miracle, the paramedics insisted on a hospital check-up. Walking through the hospital, I was met with

THE BEGINNING

the astonished gazes of nurses and doctors. Yet, within two hours, I was discharged and back in my own bed.

Reflecting on that day brings a flood of emotions. First and foremost, gratitude: *Thank You, Jesus, for healing me.* But it also brings questions: Why me? Why did God intervene in my life at that moment? These are questions that haunted me for thirty years, questions I still struggle with.

For a long time, I felt almost ashamed of this miraculous event, keeping it hidden even from those closest to me. It felt too vast, too raw to share. Also, since that day, my life hasn't been all rainbows and butterflies. I've encountered many hardships associated with my accident since the day of my miracle. Navigating life with a brain injury from such a young age definitely led me into situations I had no business being in. I've battled physical and mental health, with bouts of chronic stress, depression, and anxiety so severe they landed me in the ER.

With help, I'm no longer ashamed to share the full story of who I am. I believe vulnerability is one of the most powerful things we can offer, not only to ourselves but to others. With that said, I try to be as honest and open as I can. But through all those difficult seasons, I never questioned Jesus's love for me. I might have felt ashamed, but I always knew where my help came from.

In Psalm 121:1-2, King David declares, "I lift my eyes toward the mountains. Where will my help come from? My help comes from the LORD, the Maker of heaven and earth."

Even in the darkest moments, I knew He was the one sustaining me. Since that day, my life has been more than just my own. While God has granted me the freedom to choose my path, deep down, I know what I am called to do—I am called to live out a mission and encourage all people to do the same. A mission that demonstrates true love. That day taught me how swiftly life can change, and it has driven me to live with purpose and urgency.

Each of us has a purpose, intricately woven into the fabric of our being by the hands of the divine. As we navigate through the chapters of our lives, we unravel more about this purpose, learning not just about life but about ourselves and the profound love that guides us. This

THE BEGINNING

question beckons us to delve deeper into the essence of our existence and embrace the mission laid out for us by our Creator. It's a journey of discovering the richness of a life lived not just for us but for a greater cause. I am so grateful to have the daily opportunity to be alive.

CHAPTER 2
THE CALL

THE CALL

If you've spent time reflecting on your purpose or place in the world, you've likely heard the term "calling" in one form or another. As I worked on this book, I began to ask myself if we truly understand what that word means. I don't ask this to challenge anyone's understanding but rather to bring clarity to those who might not fully grasp what a "calling" is or how it fits into their everyday life.

In many circles, few concepts carry as much weight as "the calling." It's often seen as a unique, deeply personal purpose that gives meaning and direction to someone's life. But here's what I've come to understand: this idea of a calling isn't confined to certain roles or professions—it applies to everyone. Whether you consider yourself a person of faith or not, the sense of being drawn toward a purpose greater than yourself is something we all can experience and explore.

Over the years, I've observed that many people make life decisions based on what they perceive as their "calling." Too often, this idea becomes narrowly tied to specific roles—whether it's leading a project, teaching, or taking on a leadership position in a particular community. While

THE PROJECT

those roles are valuable, I want to challenge the notion that a calling is confined to a title or position. It goes far beyond a specific role and is something each of us carries into every part of our lives.

To me, our true calling is about living with purpose and following the principles Jesus taught. It's not about waiting for a grand moment to reveal your purpose; it's about how we live each day—showing love, caring for those in need, forgiving others, and making a positive difference in the lives of those around us. For those who follow Jesus, this includes the call to share His message and live in alignment with His teachings.

In John 14:15, Jesus says, "If you love me, you will keep my commands". This call isn't tied to a specific role or profession—it's an invitation to a way of life. It's not confined to church walls or religious titles but is found in the way we treat others, the way we serve our communities, and the way we love—even when it's difficult.

Whether or not you share my faith, the idea of living with love, compassion, and a commitment to something greater than ourselves can resonate deeply. For me, living out what Jesus commanded is how I walk in my calling, and I believe that same sense of purpose can inspire and guide anyone seeking to live a meaningful life.

This isn't a new revelation for me. In fact, I've carried this understanding for as long as I can remember—I truly love people. I'm one of those crazy extroverts who feels affirmed and energized simply by being around others. I know we can all be a lot to handle sometimes, but there's something about people that captivates me. There's a beauty in people, in their stories, in their struggles and triumphs, that makes me want to be present with them, to serve them, and to show them love.

This deep concern for others, which took root in me at a young age, became the driving force behind my desire to serve. It shaped my passion for living a mission-focused life—one dedicated to making a meaningful difference in the lives of those around me. That passion came full circle on Tuesday, January 12, 2010.

That was the day a devastating earthquake struck Haiti, forever altering the course of the nation—and my life. The summer before the earthquake, I visited Haiti for

THE PROJECT

the first time, and it changed me. I fell in love with the people—not just because they were my father's people, but because I experienced firsthand how true connection transcends culture, race, and nationality. It comes from a genuine understanding and love for others.

This experience taught me something I'll never forget—the power of human connection, especially with those who may look different from you or come from a different place. When we open our hearts to truly see and value one another, we begin to break down barriers and discover the beauty of our shared humanity. That connection has the power to transform not just relationships but entire lives, including our own. So, when tragedy struck on that fateful day, it felt deeply personal.

On that tragic day, a 7.0 magnitude earthquake struck near Port-au-Prince, and within seconds, lives were shattered. Over 230,000 people were killed, nearly 300,000 were injured, and more than 1.5 million were left homeless. The devastation was beyond comprehension—entire neighborhoods flattened, hospitals and schools reduced to rubble, and the already struggling infrastructure of the country was brought to its knees. It was one

THE CALL

of the deadliest natural disasters in modern history, and the images of chaos and loss filled our TV screens as we anxiously waited for news of loved ones.

Haiti, already one of the poorest nations in the world, was now facing an unimaginable humanitarian crisis. The weight of the disaster was unbearable and made my love for the people and the country even more profound.

That night, I lay awake, the terror of what my loved ones might be enduring gnawing at me. Compelled to act, I went to school the next day and asked each of my teachers to turn on the TV for live updates on Haiti. After school, I rushed to the church where my father worked and sat in on a meeting with my parents to plan a trip to Haiti as soon as possible. We were determined to do whatever we could to help. In the midst of that urgency, one verse resonated deeply in my heart and has remained vital to my life even today: Isaiah 6:8 (NIV), where God calls out, "Whom shall I send? And who will go for us?" Isaiah responds, "Here I am. Send me!" This passage has become a personal anthem for me. Although I never envisioned myself as a full-time missionary, these

THE PROJECT

words stirred in me an intense desire to follow wherever I felt led.

Isaiah's journey began with a life-altering vision just after King Uzziah's death. At this pivotal moment, Isaiah felt unworthy, acutely aware of his imperfections and those of the people around him. Yet, through a transformative experience—when a seraph pressed a hot coal to his lips—he was cleansed and prepared to answer the call. When God asked for a messenger, Isaiah didn't hesitate. He eagerly volunteered, declaring, "Send me!" His readiness wasn't about perfection or complete preparedness—it was about having a willing heart.

Many of us can relate to Isaiah's feelings of inadequacy. Think back to times when you've felt called to do something meaningful but hesitated because of guilt, doubt, or struggles with your past or present. This internal battle is something we all face at times, and it can hold us back from stepping into a larger purpose.

In those moments of self-doubt, it's crucial to remember the power of grace and renewal. For me, as a follower of Jesus, this means trusting in His sacrifice, which makes us whole and equips us for the journey ahead. Yet, the principle remains universal—when we let go of shame and embrace our potential, we open ourselves to incredible opportunities to impact the world around us.

This narrative isn't limited to Isaiah or ancient prophets. It resonates with each of us today. The question, "Whom shall I send?" isn't just for the spiritually elite or the overtly religious—it's for anyone who feels a tug toward something bigger than themselves. It's a call to action, a call to step forward with a willing and open heart. Isaiah's response reminds us to embrace opportunities with courage, whether that means helping someone in need, supporting a cause, or even making significant life changes.

Over the past year, in moments of quiet reflection, I've learned an essential lesson: I must say **NO** to distractions to fully say **YES** to what matters most. This truth applies to everyone—believers and non-believers alike. To pursue what we're called to do, we often need to let go of competing priorities. Saying no to what pulls us away can be the most powerful step we take toward living with purpose.

THE PROJECT

A few nights after the earthquake in Haiti, I overheard my father planning to leave for the country. At that moment, I felt an undeniable pull to join him. With a heartfelt prayer, I whispered those words, "Here I am. Send me." And He certainly did.

I can still recall it as if it were yesterday—rising at 5 a.m., the sky still dark, while I gathered my things to meet a small group at the church. It was a diverse mix: a few pastors, a United States Army Captain, a journalist, and me, all united by a single purpose—to drive to Miami and, hopefully, make our way into Haiti. The plan was far from certain, but we had faith. The earthquake had decimated the country, and we knew we had to be there. Something inside me stirred during that journey—a deep, undeniable awakening in my soul.

We arrived in Miami late at night. The airport felt strange, buzzing with people but filled with a quiet sense of tension. After hours of struggling to secure transportation into Haiti, we realized we would be spending the night on the cold airport floor. It was a long and restless night. As I lay there, a flood of questions kept surging through my mind: *Why am I here? What can I possibly offer? Am I ready*

THE CALL

for this? These weren't just thoughts—they were doubts. I was only seventeen, volunteering to enter a disaster zone. Most kids my age were thinking about prom and college applications, but I was in an airport, about to step into one of the worst natural disasters the world has ever seen. Still, despite the uncertainty, I could feel something growing inside me—a thirst for adventure, yes, but also a deep sense of responsibility and purpose. For the first time in my life, I knew I was exactly where I was meant to be.

The next day, my father and the team worked tirelessly to secure our way into Haiti. Hours later, a deal was made, and we finally boarded the plane and took off. I was emotionally exhausted and quickly fell asleep, the anticipation still buzzing in my mind. As the plane began its descent into Haiti, I was jolted awake by something unexpected. It wasn't the sound of the plane but a smell—something I had never encountered before. Yes, you heard me right—we could smell it from the air. It wasn't just the scent of destruction; it was deeper than that. In that moment, everything became real. The headlines, the stories, the images—they were no longer distant. I was about to step into them. And with that realization,

THE PROJECT

doubts came flooding back: *What am I doing here?! How can I possibly make a difference?!* As we began to land, an overwhelming sense of darkness hit me. It wasn't just physical—something more spiritual, almost oppressive, clung to the air. For those who have never been to Haiti, it's hard to describe. It's not the people, but something about the place—the weight of centuries of struggle, of poverty, of spiritual warfare—hangs in the air, almost palpable. Landing there, you don't just see the devastation; you feel it in your bones. People live with this reality daily, but for me, it was a new and heavy burden, one I wasn't sure I could carry.

I've always struggled with fear, but this wasn't ordinary fear. It was something darker, something that felt like oppression. The fear pressed down on me. It was hard to breathe, and my mind filled with doubts and anxieties. It wasn't just the physical devastation I was walking into; it was the spiritual battle raging all around me. I had a choice. I could let this fear crush me, or I could fight it with the only weapon I knew—my faith and the Word of God.

Before we landed and the plane door swung open, I had already made my decision. This was a spiritual

THE CALL

battleground, and I had to step into it with the heart of a soldier. The weight of this place pressed on me—not to break me, but to open my eyes to the burdens these people carried every single day. It wasn't about me; it was about them. I wasn't there just to witness; I was there to serve.

I've always believed that everything happens for a reason—not in a cliché or superficial way, but as a choice. A choice to believe that even in the hardest moments, there can be purpose and hope. So, I embraced that moment, not as a passive observer, but as someone ready to make a difference. I stepped off that plane with a mission: to bring light into a place overwhelmed by darkness.

THE DESTRUCTION

As the airplane door opened, the scene before me was anything but ordinary. The humid air hit me like a wave—thick, oppressive, and filled with a mix of jet fuel, sweat, and an unsettling undertone of something burning. Stepping off the plane, I found myself in a surreal moment, surrounded by military personnel and massive airplanes. It was like a scene from a movie, but this was no Hollywood set—this was raw, unfiltered reality.

The sight of the colossal military planes parked on the runway left an indelible mark on my memory. At just seventeen years old and having had no prior exposure to the United States military, the sight was awe-inspiring and surreal. The sheer size and power of the aircraft, combined with the urgency and intensity of the situation, made it a moment I will never forget. Soldiers were everywhere, moving with purpose, guiding people in and out, managing the supplies being flown into the island.

As we continued along on the runway, I noticed it wasn't only the United States military that was present; there were multiple countries represented. At that moment, I

THE PROJECT

realized that the whole world was here, coming together to respond to this crisis. It was a powerful reminder of the global impact of natural disasters and the importance of unity in times of need.

We were quickly ushered towards the lobby of the airport, the air thick with noise and darkness. The atmosphere was charged with frenetic energy—the kind that makes your heart race and your senses sharpen. Looking out onto the island, I could see numerous fires burning in the distance. The orange glow against the darkened sky was both haunting and mesmerizing.

As we made our way to our designated area, we were met by our ride and welcome crew. Their presence was a reassuring sight amidst the chaos. We quickly loaded our supplies onto the truck and prepared to head out.

It was a moment filled with excitement and anticipation. My heart was pumping with the thrill of being part of such a significant event. However, doubt crept into my mind. *I'm not a soldier*, I thought. *I have no money to give, no influence or wisdom to offer. I'm just a young man; what can I possibly do to make a difference?*

THE DESTRUCTION

Have you ever found yourself in a similar moment, questioning what you have to offer in a challenging situation?

These questions arise because doubt is a thief, robbing us of the confidence to follow God's command.

Doubt can profoundly affect our sense of purpose and our ability to live out a meaningful life. It makes us question our abilities, the values we hold dear, or even the existence of something greater than ourselves. This doubt can lead to a lack of confidence in sharing our beliefs or pursuing what we feel called to do, holding us back from connecting with others or making a difference. It can also cause us to hesitate or resist following the guidance we sense within us. Ultimately, doubt weakens our resolve and keeps us from fully embracing the principles and values that give our lives purpose and direction.

As we drove through the streets of Haiti, the devastation caused by the earthquake was utterly incomprehensible.

Picture cascading rows of falling dominos, meticulously set up to tumble one after another. Now imagine

THE PROJECT

those dominoes were real homes—homes upon homes upon homes, all completely demolished and stacked atop one another.

The scene was overwhelming. I will never forget the rubble and wreckage that stretched as far as the eye could see, each pile potentially hiding someone fighting for their life beneath. The sheer scale of destruction was beyond anything I had imagined. My words cannot fully convey the magnitude of what we witnessed that night.

As we continued our drive through the city, the fires I had seen from the airport took on a chilling new reality. Drawing closer, I realized they were funeral pyres—bodies burning, the air thick with grief, and the scent of smoke. It was a haunting scene. Every night, in the aftermath of unimaginable loss, families had no choice but to cremate their loved ones in the open air, right before their own eyes.

The shock of seeing a deceased body for the first time hit me hard, but more profound was realizing the daily struggle these people faced. The countless fires I

THE DESTRUCTION

had spotted from the airport were not mere flames—they were daily farewell rites for the departed, a stark reminder of the unrelenting grief and hardship endured by the Haitian people.

This experience in Haiti was a stark departure from my previous visit, where I had been surrounded by beauty and tranquility. Now, the landscape was marred by total devastation, casting a shadow of incomprehensible destruction. Buildings lay in ruins, their skeletal remains jutting out like the bones of a decaying beast. Streets were filled with debris, making navigation a perilous task. The once vibrant neighborhoods were now ghostly remnants of their former selves, filled with the echoes of the past.

In the midst of this devastation, doubt crept in again. *How could I, a young person with no experience in disaster relief, pastoral ministry, or military expertise, possibly make a difference here?*

In my moment of uncertainty, a whisper echoed in my spirit: *Go*. It was a command that resonated deeply, even amidst the chaos and despair.

THE PROJECT

Go and do what? I questioned inwardly, feeling overwhelmed by the enormity of the task.

Again, the answer came: *Go.* As I looked out over the destruction, I recalled Jesus's commission to His disciples in Matthew 28:19 (NIV) to "Go and make disciples of all nations." Suddenly, the weight of the call became clear. These people didn't need sermons; they needed love. The island was ablaze with suffering and displacement. Yet, in the midst of my doubts, a gentle reminder surfaced: *He is all they need. Their true help comes from the Lord.*

At that moment, all uncertainty dissolved. I understood my role: to be a vessel of the Lord, embodying the love and compassion of Jesus amidst the devastation. It wasn't about grand gestures or eloquent speeches. It was about living out the commandment by loving and serving these hurting people.

Thus, I set out as a servant, offering what I could—comfort, aid, and the assurance of love.

THE DESTRUCTION

As we turned into the compound, what we witnessed left us speechless. As the gates opened into the orphanage, we were met with a heart-wrenching sight—over 300 people scattered across the grounds. They were sleeping wherever they could find space, on cut-out cardboard boxes and makeshift sleeping bags. The people ranged from tiny infants to the elderly, all huddled together in this sanctuary for the displaced. Seeing the place where my father grew up, now serving as a refuge, was deeply emotional, to say the least. In my Western mindset, I had expected to see the UN or Red Cross already established, providing the Haitian people with the help they desperately needed. But that expectation was far from reality.

The truth hit hard—they had nothing and nowhere to go. No one to call, no one who could offer a spare room for the night. All they had was a cardboard box to sleep on under the open sky, surrounded by total strangers. The weight of this realization settled heavily in my heart as I began to grasp the enormity of what lay ahead.

As the night wore on, we quickly realized the vast amount of work that needed to be done. We unpacked our

THE PROJECT

belongings and headed to the office where we would be staying. We stayed in a room about the size of a 10x20 storage unit—cramped and sparse. I remember that first night vividly. I couldn't sleep, of course—fear and excitement had me wide awake. I lay on the floor next to my dad when suddenly, I heard the steady beat of a drum in the distance. In my ignorance, I thought maybe someone was having a party, but then my dad began to pray. I was confused—why would he be praying? Then it dawned on me. Those beats we heard weren't from a celebration; they were from a voodoo priest leading a ritual. They were seeking the devil's help in the wake of so much loss.

Imagine everything you've ever heard about good and evil—the timeless stories, the epic battles between the hero and the villain that we see in movies and books. Now, imagine that the movie isn't just fiction but your reality. Imagine finding yourself in the middle of an actual battle between good and evil. That was the realization that hit me that night. This wasn't some far-off tale my father used to tell us as kids. This was real, and I was right in the thick of it.

THE DESTRUCTION

As those drums continued to beat into the night, I found myself questioning how anyone could choose voodoo as their form of religion. It seemed like such a dark and hopeless way to view the world. But as I lay there, reflecting on the history and the circumstances of the people who practiced it, I began to understand. Voodoo is often practiced in areas of extreme poverty, with Haiti being one of the most prominent examples. The people worshiping that night were desperate. They had lost everything they had, which was so little to begin with. Now, surrounded by total destruction and death, with no visible hope for the future, they were searching for anything that might offer them a semblance of control or comfort.

It's easy to pass judgment on these people, to question their hearts and wonder if they truly understand the impact of what they're doing to their souls. But what I realized was that if they were in such deep despair, then what better time to show them the true light of the world?

The judgment I felt rising in my heart served as a stark reminder. As a young man, I've often noticed the

THE PROJECT

amount of judgment some "Christians" pass. It always confused me—the divisive language I'd hear directed at certain people. It's curious how some can proclaim their love for all of God's children yet so easily forget who those people are and what they look like. A double standard has crept into our culture—as long as we say the right things, we think we're doing just fine. But Jesus never taught that. He commanded us to love our neighbors as ourselves!

That night, I realized that my actions, though admirable to some, meant nothing if I didn't have the right heart—the heart to see these people the way He does, the heart to serve as a humble servant, not as a savior.

The next morning was quite the adventure! Of course, we were woken up by a rooster crowing as loud as he could (quite the alarm clock, haha!). The people in the compound were eager to meet us and discuss plans to help the community. We quickly got ready and began setting up a distribution center. Our goal was simple: feed, clothe, and treat. If there were any individuals with severe injuries, we wanted to ensure they could be transported

THE DESTRUCTION

to the city where the UN and Red Cross were actively treating people.

So, we started making our rounds, taking note of all the issues these people were facing. My job was to bring JOY! My role was to play with the kids while their parents discussed their needs with the others. And let me tell you, this role was an absolute blast! Not knowing the language, I was a bit nervous—how in the world would I keep these kids engaged and connected? But you know what? You'd be surprised how far a smile can go!

As the day went on, it became clear that what we had wouldn't be enough. Someone mentioned a headquarters where all the humanitarian relief organizations were based, so we decided to head into town and see if they could help us better serve these people. That drive was one I'll never forget. About an hour in, I realized we had entered a place that words can hardly describe. After the earthquake hit Haiti, the island was left in ruins, forcing its people to create something called "Tent City." As we entered Tent City, the sheer magnitude of what I was seeing took my breath away. Imagine a sprawling expanse stretching as far as the eye can see, filled with

THE PROJECT

makeshift shelters cobbled together from whatever materials people could scavenge—tattered tarps, frayed cloth, rusted metal sheets, and even old cardboard. The ground beneath was a patchwork of dirt, mud, and debris, with narrow, winding paths worn down by the countless feet that had trudged through.

The tents themselves were cramped and crowded, haphazardly clustered together with barely enough space to walk between them. It felt as if the entire city had been flattened and compressed into this chaotic maze. People were everywhere—men, women, children—all packed together in a sea of desperation. Some tents were nothing more than a few sticks holding up a piece of cloth, barely offering any real shelter from the elements. The air was thick with the smell of sweat, smoke, and the faint, acrid scent of waste. Here and there, small fires flickered where people were cooking whatever meager food they could find. Children, some clothed in little more than rags, played in the dirt, their laughter a stark contrast to the grim surroundings. A constant hum of activity filled the air—people talking, crying, shouting—interspersed with the occasional wail of someone in deep distress.

THE DESTRUCTION

As I looked around, the scale of it all was overwhelming. It felt as if the very fabric of humanity had been torn apart, and this was what remained—a desperate attempt to survive amidst the ruins. The scene was a jarring reminder of the fragility of life and the resilience of the human spirit, all at once. This was Tent City, a place where over 1.5 million souls clung to hope in the midst of utter devastation.

As we traveled through the city, witnessing more devastation and loss, we came across the famous statue Le Marron Inconnu. This powerful bronze figure depicts a nearly naked slave fugitive, kneeling on one knee with his torso arched and a broken chain on his left ankle. He holds a conch shell to his lips, head tilted upward as if to blow it, while his other hand grips a machete by his right ankle. The statue, a revered symbol of black liberation, commemorates the rallying cry that sparked the Haitian Revolution and the abolition of slavery.

Seeing this statue was an emotional moment for me, not just because of its historical significance, but also because it held a personal connection. Growing up, I had a small wooden carving of this very statue on my

THE PROJECT

bedroom dresser. It symbolized so many things for me—freedom, resilience, and the strength of my heritage. But now, seeing it in this context, covered in clothes and used as a drying rack, hit me hard. I wasn't upset at the people; it was just another sobering reminder of how devastating this situation truly was.

When we finally reached the hub of the humanitarian organizations, the scene was as overwhelming as the devastation we'd witnessed throughout the day. The headquarters was heavily secured, with fences, military personnel, and rows of massive trailers and tents stocked with supplies. We were directed from one official to the next, finally getting a chance to speak on behalf of our community in desperate need. Grateful for the promise that a shipment would be sent within twenty-four hours, I couldn't ignore the uneasy feeling settling in my gut.

As I looked around, the stark contrast between those inside the hub and those outside was jarring. Just hours before, I had seen families crammed into makeshift tents with nothing but the clothes on their backs. Now, here I stood, surrounded by mountains of supplies behind a fence, guarded and protected—supplies that weren't reaching the people who needed them most, and certainly not fast enough.

It became clear that the aid process was tangled in red tape, more political than practical. Bureaucracy slowed everything down, and the people suffering the most—the ones living in unimaginable conditions—were left waiting. I understand there are systems and procedures that need to be followed, but what I saw was heartbreaking. It wasn't just about logistics; it felt like the real urgency, the human lives at stake, had gotten lost in the shuffle. Aid wasn't reaching those on the ground who needed it now. That day, I saw the darker side of humanitarian work. While humanity has the capacity for incredible love and generosity, there's also the temptation to let politics and power structures take precedence. Much of the aid was caught up in bureaucracy—transactional and slow to move. But we can't allow systems to overshadow the people who need help the most. There are lives at stake, and no amount of paperwork or protocol should stand in the way of that.

THE PROJECT

This same mindset shows up in our everyday lives. Decisions are often delayed or complicated by layers of bureaucracy. As I've grown older, I've realized that this is how our society tends to operate—we see needs right in front of us, yet we're told to go through "systems," "organizations," or even rely on someone else's approval before taking action.

But when you look at the core teachings of compassion and service, the message is clear: we're called to act. Helping those in need—feeding the hungry, clothing the naked, caring for the sick—isn't something to put off or leave to others. It's a responsibility we all share. As the saying goes, "What we do for the least among us, we do for something far greater than ourselves."

When we recognize what's right and what needs to be done, it's on us to step forward. The mission to make a difference doesn't belong to someone else—it belongs to each of us. The choice to act, to care, and to change the world starts with you.

CHAPTER 4
THE MOMENT

THE MOMENT

As we returned to the compound, I found myself battling a wave of emotions after our visit to the humanitarian headquarters. Frustration, disappointment, helplessness—they all swirled together, leaving me unsure of how to process what I had seen. I wanted to escape those feelings, even just for a little while, so I decided to spend time with the children who were playing near the concrete soccer field.

It was late in the day, around 6:00 p.m., and the sun was beginning to set. Laughter and energy filled the air as the kids played with a joy that seemed almost impossible given their circumstances. Their resilience was humbling, and for a moment, I felt lighter—almost rejuvenated—just by being near them. But then, out of the corner of my eye, I noticed a baby girl, probably no more than a year old, sitting quietly by herself. She wasn't playing or crying, just sitting there alone, watching. I couldn't stop looking at her. Something about her stillness stood out in stark contrast to the chaos around us. After an hour or so, I noticed an eight-year-old boy approach her. He gently picked her up and carried her to a mattress that had been set up outside. She clung to him tightly, and within minutes, she was asleep in his arms. I sat there,

THE PROJECT

waiting for an adult to come, but as the evening darkened, no one did.

That night, I couldn't sleep. I lay on my air mattress, staring at the ceiling, consumed by worry. How could an eight-year-old possibly protect her? What if she wandered off or someone took her? The thought of her tiny, vulnerable face kept me awake all night. By morning, I knew I couldn't just sit idly by. I had to do something.

I went back to the same spot, and there she was—sitting on the same mattress, watching the older kids play. I rummaged through my bag and found a pack of peanut butter crackers. Kneeling down, I offered them to her. Her eyes lit up as she grabbed them and devoured them quickly. I realized she probably hadn't eaten a decent meal in days. That simple act—sharing food—felt like the most natural thing in the world, but it also felt sacred, as if something far greater was happening in that moment.

Looking back now, I see that moment for what it truly was: a connection, a breaking down of barriers, and an act of compassion that changed me more than it could have ever changed her. Sharing those crackers

THE MOMENT

reminded me of something profound. Throughout His time on earth, Jesus often used the act of breaking bread to connect with people on a deeper level. Whether it was feeding the multitudes or sitting at a table with His disciples, He showed us that sometimes the simplest gestures carry the most meaning.

It wasn't just about feeding her; it was about meeting her where she was. At that moment, it didn't matter what was "appropriate" or whether I was overstepping. What mattered was love in action.

That experience has stayed with me for over fifteen years. At the time, I was just 17, but for the first time, I understood what it meant to feel a fatherly love—a deep, protective instinct that overwhelmed me. I remember bawling uncontrollably on the tarmac as we waited to board the plane. It felt as though I was abandoning her. My mind raced with questions: "How could she be so alone? Why wasn't anyone there to protect her? Could I somehow adopt her?"

And then it hit me. That overwhelming love I felt for her—it was just a fraction of how God loves us. That night, I

THE PROJECT

understood in a new way how deeply God longs for us to stay close to Him, how He aches when we're lost or vulnerable. It was a love so profound that He gave His Son for us, so we'd never be abandoned.

Years later, as I reflect on that moment, I realize it wasn't just the baby girl who needed someone. I needed her, too. She reminded me of what it truly means to serve—not for recognition or results, but because love compels us to act.

For six years, I served in full-time ministry, but somewhere along the way, I lost sight of that truth. I became consumed by performance, by the pressure to grow, please, and succeed. I forgot the simple joy of following Jesus and loving people in the way He calls us to. In the Western church, it's so easy to get caught up in the systems and traditions—polishing sermons, perfecting worship services, expanding buildings—that we lose sight of the heart of the Gospel.

Caring for that baby girl reminded me that service isn't about accolades or visible results. It's about stepping into the moment and loving with no strings attached. That's the kind of love Jesus showed us—a love that

THE MOMENT

doesn't wait for recognition or a transaction. It's about seeing the need in front of you and doing something about it, no matter how small the act may seem.

I don't know what happened to that little girl, and I probably never will. But I choose to believe that those few days of care—those peanut butter crackers—made a difference, even if only in a small way. I cling to the hope that one day, we'll meet again in heaven, and she'll know how much she taught me about love.

As I think back to that trip, I am reminded of what pure and undefiled religion looks like: caring for the least of these, as James 1:27 so beautifully puts it. It's not about comfort or recognition; it's about surrender. It's about being willing to step into the hard places and love unconditionally, trusting that God will use our small acts to build His kingdom.

I pray that my life is marked by that kind of love—a love that doesn't need a transaction, a thank-you, or even an acknowledgment. It's a love that simply sees the need and responds. Because in God's eyes, it's the smallest acts, done with the greatest love, that truly matter.

CHAPTER 5

THE PLATE PROJECT

Many years passed, and I received a phone call from my father. Our beloved Grand Moon, my dad's mother, had received her gift of eternity. I felt a sense of joy hearing the news, knowing that she was no longer burdened by the hardships of this world but blessed with her Savior's gift of eternity. Yet, along with that joy, I felt a familiar stirring in my heart.

My dad told me that he and my mother were planning to head to Haiti in a few days to give Grand Moon a memorial. Without hesitation, I asked if I could join them, realizing how long it had been since I last set foot in Haiti.

Upon arriving in Haiti, I met with my parents to see our family and begin the memorial celebrations. But I felt disconnected, as if I had drifted from the mission that was always placed in my heart. By this point in my life, I had graduated college, gotten married, and welcomed my first child. At twenty-seven years old, I found myself selfishly focused on my plans and ambitions, forgetting the deep connection I had to this place.

THE PROJECT

Yet, as I stood there, I realized this trip would be about much more than celebrating my grandmother's life, though that was incredibly important. I sensed a deeper calling unfolding—a reminder of the mission I had once embraced.

During our stay, one particular walk would forever shape my understanding of the mission before me. I'll never forget leaving our hotel and walking down an alley when, all of a sudden, I saw piles of garbage everywhere. As we moved closer to this huge terrain, I noticed dogs, chickens, and wild pigs scavenging through the scraps. Then, I thought I saw something else—a small figure among the animals. I blinked, hoping I was just imagining it. But as we drew nearer, my worst fears were confirmed. Among those animals was a child.

I want you to picture this: in a pit of trash, children were rummaging through the piles, hoping to find even a morsel to fill their empty stomachs. My throat tightened; tears welled up in my eyes as the reality of hunger in this community hit me hard. As we continued walking through this terrain of trash, I couldn't help but picture my own beautiful baby girl, Shiloh. The love I have for my daughter goes beyond words, and I know many parents reading this will understand exactly what I mean. You would do anything for your child to make sure they have food in their belly.

There's a misconception some of us Americans have—that parents in Haiti, or in any poverty-stricken country, don't care for their babies. I want to shed light on that ignorance. Here's the truth: in the severe grip of poverty, when a child reaches a certain age, they are left on their own, not because of a lack of love but because there simply isn't enough for everyone. It becomes a matter of survival. Love has nothing to do with it; it's about life or death.

Now, with that understanding, imagine this being your everyday reality. Imagine your beautiful children, the ones you would do anything for, and having to choose daily between keeping yourself alive or them. They eat, or you eat. Many of us might think, *That's easy; I would choose my children.* But in America, we sometimes can't even choose our children over our own selfish ambitions. This is the type of poverty we witnessed

THE PROJECT

that day—a child reaching an age where they were completely on their own.

Words can't fully capture the shock that ran through my body, seeing what I saw that day. To look into a child's eyes and see the desperate nature of survival brought me right back to a little girl I saw many years ago. The uncertainty of their day-to-day life is what drives me to be an advocate for the rest of my life. No child should have to worry about where their next meal will come from. No child should have to sift through garbage alongside dogs and pigs just to find scraps. This stark reality reminds us how vital it is to bring light into the darkest places. Light doesn't fight against darkness; it simply exists, and by its very presence, darkness fades. In a similar way, hope and love can transform even the most desperate situations.

Just as light reveals what is hidden and brings clarity, love has the power to bring comfort and reassurance where fear and despair once thrived. It doesn't waver, even in the deepest shadows—it shines, steady and unchanging. It reminds us that peace and hope are always possible, even in the hardest moments.

THE PLATE PROJECT

That day in Haiti, as I looked around, I realized our role wasn't to fix every problem or solve every struggle. Instead, our purpose was to bring hope where there was despair, to offer love where it was missing, and to be a steady presence in the midst of overwhelming challenges. It's about being part of something greater— helping light shine where it's needed most.

This was the moment I finally understood what my parents had been doing my whole life. From the outside, it's easy to think that all their service amounted to nothing, given the overwhelming needs of this country and its people. But my dad would always say, "If it's only one, then it's worth it—because at one point, I was the one. And if it weren't for someone serving me, I wouldn't be standing here today. And if I'm not standing here, then you aren't, and if you aren't here, then your beautiful babies aren't either. You see, one faithful servant can truly change generations."

It was at that moment I realized what my role would be. I knew I was meant to support and encourage my parents—who were already making a difference by feeding 15 to 30 children from this area three days a week out

THE PROJECT

of our family's home. My calling was clear: to help share their mission with the world.

After seeing the overwhelming need, I knew it was time to serve alongside them and help blossom this movement, inviting others to join us on this journey. This is what we now call The Plate Project—changing lives one meal at a time!

At The Plate Project, our vision is to create a dependable safe haven where individuals are not only fed but also feel valued, protected, and seen. We believe that changing lives starts with meeting basic needs and extending love and dignity to those we serve.

Growing up, I watched my parents pour their hearts into serving the Haitian community, often with just a few resources but a whole lot of faith. From feeding children to offering support to struggling families, their efforts taught me that it isn't about how much you have but how much love you're willing to give. This is the heart of The Plate Project—an extension of that same love, scaled to reach as many as we can.

THE PLATE PROJECT

As a mission-based movement, the Plate Project is committed to alleviating hunger and improving the well-being of children across the world! We operate multiple community kitchens that provide nutritious meals to those living in some of the world's most impoverished areas. But each meal we serve is more than just food—it's a message of hope.

Our mission goes beyond feeding. The Plate Project is dedicated to protecting and empowering communities. We strive to equip families with the tools they need to achieve self-sufficiency and transform their own lives. Our aim is to help individuals build a sustainable future and break free from the cycle of poverty.

We stand firmly against the dehumanizing oppression that affects these communities, driven by our belief that everyone deserves to live with dignity and security. I remember standing in the streets of Tent City, overwhelmed by the sheer scale of need. Yet, in that place of despair, I also saw incredible resilience. This is why we keep going—because there is a light that cannot be extinguished, even by the darkest circumstances.

THE PROJECT

Our work is inspired by the words of Jesus: "For I was hungry and you gave me something to eat, I was thirsty and you gave me something to drink, I was a stranger and you invited me in" (Matthew 25:35, NIV). This teaching compels us to reach out, serve those in need, and embody Christ's love through our actions. When we share a meal or offer a kind word, we say, "You are seen, you are loved, and you are not alone." We have a huge vision for the future and truly believe we are entrusted to build a foundation beyond ourselves. Our efforts are focused on strengthening our foundation in Haiti as we prepare to go wherever the Lord calls.

I know you might be thinking, *This all sounds nice—good for you and your mission.* But let me be completely honest with you: "nice" has nothing to do with it. If I could have it any other way, I'd wish there was no need for this work at all. I'd wish for a world where suffering and pain didn't exist. I'd wish we didn't have to talk about movements like this because every child everywhere was already cared for, fed, and safe. But that's not the world we live in.

THE PLATE PROJECT

The harsh reality is that there are children dying of hunger every single day. There are children being orphaned, growing up on the streets without a family to protect them. There are children being trafficked and sold like any product you can buy at the store. And shame on us, as humans, for turning a blind eye and pretending this isn't happening.

You see, the truth is the truth, and it's time for all of us to rise up and act with everything inside of us, to do what needs to be done. These children have no voice. So, let's be their voice! Yes, I am asking for you to join us on our mission to feed the children all over the world, to change a life one meal at a time!

At its core, The Plate Project was birthed from a profound desire to see the people restored back to health. We believe that feeding the body is essential, but feeding the soul is eternal. As Jesus said in John 6:35, "I am the bread of life. . . . No one who comes to me will ever be hungry, and no one who believes in me will ever be thirsty again." Our mission is to provide both physical sustenance and spiritual nourishment, helping people find lasting hope and restoration.

THE PROJECT

And isn't this the kind of mission we're meant to embrace? I often think about how much the world needs hope—a hope that goes beyond fleeting moments or shallow pursuits. My heart aches for those who don't know the depth of meaning that can be found in a life connected to something greater. For so many, life feels like a cycle of going through the motions, numb to purpose or destiny, wondering when it all will end.

I can't help but feel a deep sadness for those weighed down by fear and anxiety, trying to manufacture joy from within, never realizing there's a greater source outside of themselves. And then there are the children—starving, abandoned, forgotten by those meant to care for them. Their faces stay with me, a reminder of how deeply broken this world is.

What the world needs most, I think, are people willing to live with humility and purpose—people who are willing to step aside from their own desires and take up something far bigger. I'm reminded of these words: "For whoever wants to save his life will lose it, but whoever loses his life because of me will find it." (Matthew 16:25, CSB). They've challenged me time and again to reexamine what it means to live with open hands, trusting that real fulfillment comes from giving myself fully to something greater.

We are all a *project*, a complicated creation full of wants and desires—the need to be loved and protected, the hope to be healed and delivered. But beyond all that, we are also called to something greater, something beyond our individual needs. We are invited to be part of God's unfolding story, a mission that extends far beyond our own lives. Each of us, with all our flaws and imperfections, a *project*. The same God who heals our wounds and quiets our fears is the One who calls us to join in loving and serving others.

As we journey through this life, navigating its joys and struggles, we must remember that our ultimate purpose lies not in the pursuit of personal comfort but in obedience to the call. Whether it's feeding the hungry or simply being present in the lives of those around us, every small act of love and service contributes to the expansion of His kingdom.

So, as this book comes to a close, the *mission continues*.

THE PROJECT

We are all works in progress—projects in the hands of a loving Creator. My prayer is that you leave these pages feeling inspired to live boldly, love deeply, and walk faithfully in your purpose. Because, in the end, it's not about perfection; it's about the journey, the obedience, and the impact we make along the way. I leave you with this one question—a question to carry with you, to wrestle with, and to answer not just with your words, but with your life:

Are you partaking in the mission?

RESOURCES

BOOK:

Orphan With a Crown by my mother, Jennifer Williams: A powerful story that will inspire readers to see God's purpose and plan for every child, especially the most vulnerable.

ORGANIZATIONS:

The Plate Project: Dedicated to serving children and families around the world through feeding programs, changing lives one meal at a time. For more information or to get involved, scan the QR code.

THE PROJECT

Old Chapel: At Old Chapel, we're about creating meaningful  connections and building community through a variety of missions. Inspired by the life of Jesus, who valued love, inclusion, and compassion, we aim to embody those principles in everything we do.

Visit oldchapel.co for more information.

PODCAST AND DIGITAL CONTENT

Old Chapel Podcast: Join us as we discuss what it means to live a life on mission. Encouraging and challenging content, featuring real, raw, and honest conversations about life and how it shapes our entire being—mind, body, and spirit.

The iconic *Le Marron Inconnu* statue in Haiti—a symbol of freedom and resilience."

The ruins of the *Cathedral of Our Lady of the Assumption, Port-au-Prince*, often called *Port-au-Prince Cathedral*.

The precious baby girl—her eyes hold a story deeper than words.

Tent City, Port-au-Prince: A stark reality following the 2010 earthquake, where thousands sought refuge and began rebuilding their lives amid immense devastation.

In the heart of Port-au-Prince after the 2010 earthquake.

"The ditch that left an indelible mark on our hearts—a place where we witnessed children scavenging for food. It became the birthplace of the Plate Project."

"The Presidential Palace in Port-au-Prince."

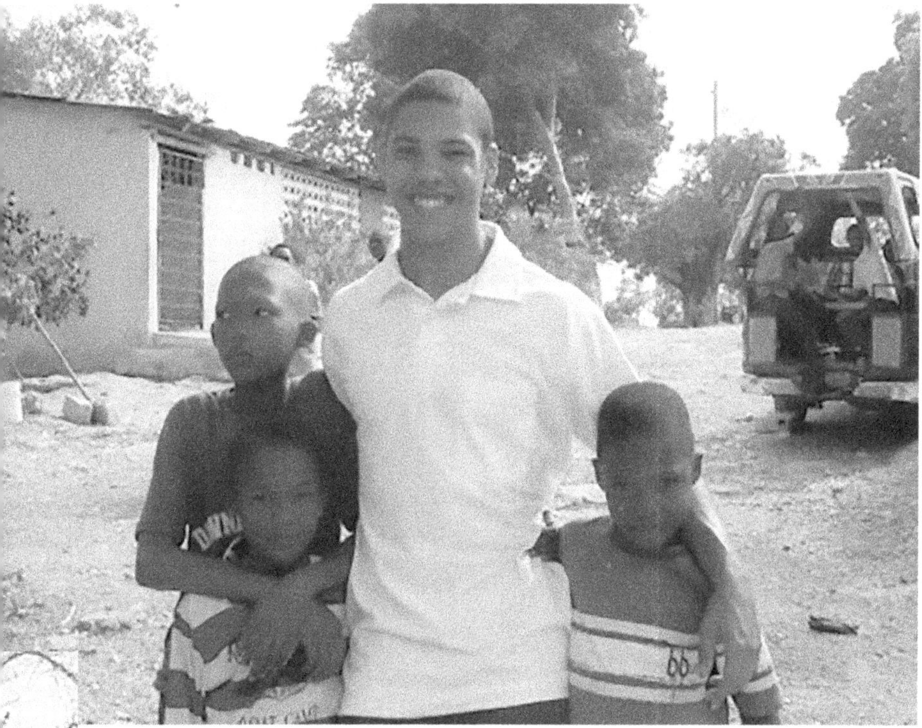

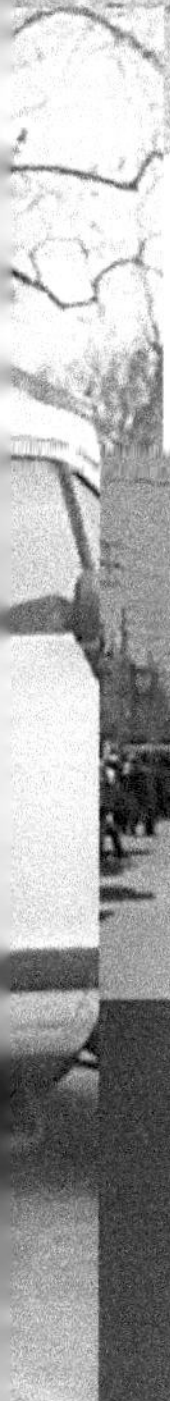

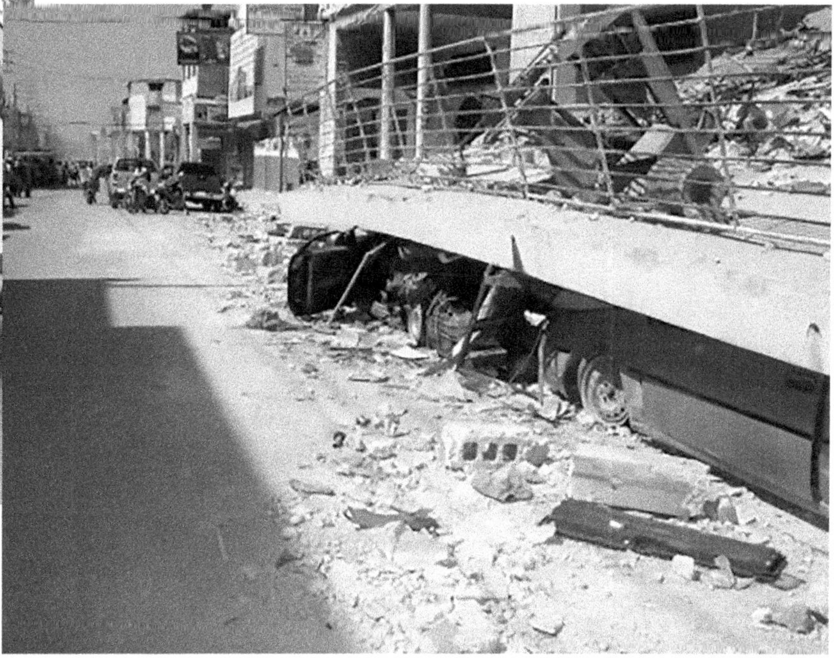

www.ingramcontent.com/pod-product-compliance
Lightning Source LLC
Chambersburg PA
CBHW062118080426
42734CB00012B/2900